Asylum Garden:
after Van Gogh

ALAN CATLIN

DOS MADRES

2020

DOS MADRES PRESS INC.
P.O.Box 294, Loveland, Ohio 45140
www.dosmadres.com   editor@dosmadres.com

Dos Madres is dedicated to the belief that the small press is essential to the vitality of contemporary literature as a carrier of the new voice, as well as the older, sometimes forgotten voices of the past. And in an ever more virtual world, to the creation of fine books pleasing to the eye and hand.

Dos Madres is named in honor of Vera Murphy and Libbie Hughes, the "Dos Madres" whose contributions have made this press possible.

Dos Madres Press, Inc. is an Ohio Not For Profit Corporation and a 501 (c) (3) qualified public charity. Contributions are tax deductible.

Executive Editor: Robert J. Murphy

Illustration & Book Design: Elizabeth H. Murphy
www.illusionstudios.net

Typeset in Adobe Garamond Pro & Dark Horse
ISBN 978-1-948017-67-1
Library of Congress Control Number: 2019953350

First Edition
Copyright 2020 Alan Catlin
All rights reserved. No part of this book may be reproduced or transmitted in any form or by any means graphic, electronic or mechanical, including photocopying, recording, taping or by any information storage or retrieval system, without the permission in writing from the publisher.
Published by Dos Madres Press, Inc.

ACKNOWLEDGEMENTS

Adam & Eve Review: Ray and His Sister and New Bride
Anthology Magazine: H. Bosch Visits Frida's Wounded Table,
Bear Creek: Haiku, Vincent 5-8 8 Aspects of Vincent
Big Windows: How We Live Now
Blue Mouse: Good Reputation Lies Sleeping
Cerberus: Diego Paints Frida's Wounded Table
Cholla Needles: Vincent 1-4 of 8 Aspects of Vincent
Creativity Webzine: Street Theater NYC, The Future
Crying Sky: The 37 Dreams of Franz Kafka
Dead Snakes: The Napier Family 1989
Diverse Voices Quarterly: Nora's Bedroom
Foliate Oak: Asylum Garden, Late Self-Portrait as Hunchback of Notre Dame
Hampden-Sydney Review: A Poem based on a Non Existent Photograph
Homestead Review: Modern Art, This Is Not Art
Ibbetson Street: Subnormals Dressed for a Halloween Masquerade
Key Satch(el): A Distance from the Sea
League of Laboring Poets: Night at the Sleepwalker's Motel
Nerve Cowboy: Cockfighter
New Verse News: Blow Up, The Year in Review in Pictures
Parting Gifts: The Vertical Movement
Pavement Saw: A Non-Existent Photograph in the Manner of Diane Arbus
Pegasus: A Non Existent Photograph in the Manner of Louis Hine
Portland Review: The Heat in the Room
Potomac Review: Reno 1949

Red Hand Press: Tammy, Rose Lee and Junior's Wedding, Day of the Dead 1932
Salvage Magazine: The Crouched Ones 1934
UFO Gigolo: Donnie with Baby and Cows, Firefighters 1935
ZYX: The Eclipse, The Artist's Reception, Fuck Picasso, A Lavender Mist

    Many of these poems appeared in different forms in the publications listed. Many thanks to the editors who gave them a home.

    And special thanks to Mary Kathryn Jablonski who encouraged me to collect them and send them in search of another home.

    With thanks to The Poet Spiel aka Tom Taylor for his Art specifically Self-Portrait of the Disease That Is Killing Me and for being who he is.

    And to Barbra Cooper for The Artist's Studio and all the art inside it.

for Valerie,
without whom none of this would have been possible

TABLE OF CONTENTS

1 - Asylum Garden

Asylum Garden 1
8 Aspects of Vincent. 2
Late Self-Portrait as Hunchback of Notre Dame.. . . 6
Grey and Gold: Chelsea Snow. 7
Self-Portrait on Isla Negra 8
"a promise built in a graveyard". 10
Dawn. 11
Night in the sleepwalker's motel. 12
Personal Demons: The Artist's Studio 13
The Artist's Reception.. 14
Diego Paints Frida Into Boschland.. 16
H. Bosch Visits Frida's Wounded Table 17
Sotheby's Shows Up at Vincent's Death Bed 19
Fuck Picasso. 20
Angels Over a Wheatfield. 21
The Locusts, The Plague, The Room 22
The Contours of Fixation 23
A Distance from the Sea 24
The Heat in the Room. 26
The Trial.. 27
A Lavender Mist 29
The 37 Dreams of Franz Kafka 30

2 - Kafka Goes to the Movies

Kafka Goes to the Movies. 33
Good Reputation Lies Sleeping 1938 35
Modern Art.. 36
A Poem Based on a Non-Existent Photograph 37
A Poem Based on a Non-Existent Photograph 38
A Poem Based on a Non-Existent Photograph 39
A Poem Based on a Non-Existent Photograph 40
A Poem Based on a Non-Existent Photograph 41
A Poem Based on a Non-Existent Photograph 42
A Poem Based on a Non-Existent Photograph 43
Non-Existent Photograph
    in the Manner of Diane Arbus 44
Non-Existent Photograph
    in the Manner of Brassai.. 45
Non-Existent Photograph
    in the Manner of Lisette Model. 46
Non-Existent Photograph
    in the Manner of Louis Hine 47
Non-Existent Photograph
    in the Manner of Weegee. 48
Non-Existent Photograph
    in the Manner of Mary Ellen Mark 49
Non-Existent Photograph
    in the Manner of Man Ray 50
Non-Existent Photograph
    in the Manner of Lupow 51
This Is Not Art 52
For Francesca Woodman Whenever I Find Her 54

3 - How We Live Now

Remains Unsuitable for Viewing 57
Self-Portrait of the Disease That Is Killing Me 58
Self-Portrait with Forensic Evidence 59
How We Live Now 60
Reno 1949 61
Donnie with Baby and Cows. 62
The Cockfighter 63
Peggy and Albert. 65
Jane, sitting for a portrait 67
Ray with Sister and New Bride 1980. 68
Annie's Kitchen 1992.. .69
Nora's Bedroom. 70
The Flyswat: The Napier Family at Home 71
Tammy. 72
The Napier Family 1989 73
Rose Lee and Junior's Wedding 75
The Crouched Ones 1934 77
Firefighters 1935. 78
Threshold 1947. 80
Day of the Dead 1932. 81
1924 82
The Eclipse 83
S. Plachy's Dachua-Germany 1985.. 84
Wladyslaw Szpilman, "The Pianist",
    with his siblings 1914. 85
The Vertical Journey: Six Movements
    Within the Heart of the City 86

Street Theater NYC 88
Subnormals Dressed for the Halloween Masquerade 89
Blow Up.. . . .. .90
The Future 91
The Year in Review in Pictures: 93

About the Author 95

- 1 -
Asylum Garden

Asylum Garden
After Van Gogh

Silent fields of
untended grass,

wild flowers and butterflies;
a brief rest between

the manic touch
of madness, of broad,

fatal brushstrokes, crows
above a field of wheat.

8 Aspects of Vincent

Vincent #1: Mistral

Asked how he painted the winds,
Vincent said, "they all have tones."

Described:
    a violet town
    star yellow
    sky blue-green
    wheat fields

Real or imagined?

Only the paintings know

Vincent #2: "The House"

that Vincent and Gauguin shared
a museum now

When the artists were in residence,
neighbors petitioned to have Vincent interred;

the fate of madmen and visionaries
everywhere,
at all times

Vincent #3: *The Prisoners 1890*

Vincent's life like this:
one of dead men walking
in exercise yard beside
insurmountable walls

This vision of his life
completed months before
he died

Vincent #4: *Kurosawa's Vincent*

A silent traveler amid all the haystacks
of the mind

Walking scant fields then up
steep, ascending path

Emerging, in the end, into vast
fields of sunflowers

Where crows ascend at the sound
of gunfire

Vincent #5: *White House at Night*

The subject was, not so much
the house, but a figure
of a man walking by, or
was he leaving the home?

He is cloaked in black
Face white
No features

Six weeks later the artist is dead

Vincent #6: *Sorrow*

Black lines on scored paper.
A naked body betrayed
Her stomach distended:
many months gone

All hope as well

Vincent #7: *Vincent's Chair*

Pipe and tobacco
resting on woven straw seat

Relics now that
the artist is dead

Vincent #8: *Rare Watercolor*

Landscape with newly
fallen snow

Dormant fields and a lone
traveler walking into head wind;

Long cold night ahead

*Late Self-Portrait
as Hunchback of Notre Dame*

after Van Gogh

His face is bloated from
an excess of alcohol and desire,

all seven sins, on a downcast
afternoon. Work cannot

alleviate the pain of wanting
what isn't there. He adds

the missing details only
he can see: the hump on his back,

a hissing harelip lisp, a swollen growth
on his neck. His lone good eye

follows you wherever you go.

Grey and Gold: Chelsea Snow
after James McNeill Whistler 1876

Odd impression
of a lone traveler

shadow in an opium
dream a kind of

non-existent man
on a street of crocodiles

Or the third man
among the bombed

out ruins of post-
war Vienna

walking toward
a receding light

barely visible
among snow swirl;

maybe not there
maybe not anywhere

at all

for Paul Pines
r.i.p.

Self-Portrait on Isla Negra

In a dream Neruda's brain is
as close as the sun on ocean
waves, on the rocks off Isla Negra,
those moss clotted perches for flocking
birds, undisturbed by words imagined
by a solitary man searching
for the elusive words he cannot seem
to speak. Everything he cannot
say is written on the walls on his home,
on the floors, the ceilings of the polished
wood, painted in script and sealed by
clear varnish anyone who desired to
could read.

Later, the swift boats come,
the cigar boats bearing secret police
disguised as acolytes seeking guidance
from the master for the hidden pathways
across turbulent seas. Instead of receiving
the knowledge he may impart, they betray
him with axes handles, spray guns, and
hammers, they use to destroy all that they
can see, turning sanctuary into madhouse,
picture windowed rooms into cages all
the elements have access to. Dreams
die here as do the dreamers riven with
despair and anger.

Arresting the master would be impolitic,
would serve no purpose they have not already
achieved. Instead, they deceive him into
believing the wine they hold out to him
is not poison but a poultice that can heal
his wounded soul.

The birds know what crime was committed here
but their language cannot be understood.

"a promise built in a graveyard"
Elizabeth Rosner

A burnt horizon like
forged metal heated by

a bright yellow sunset,
a drift of clouds casting

dream shadows on bare
trees black birds reside in

near plowed-under-for-
the-season-fields; by derelict

barn, rusted trellises are aching
for their vines.

Dawn

after Odd Nedrun

on the plain of penitents, reveals
the results of a book beyond
Revelation, pages removed for
the perpetual fires; of missing body
parts, the surgically removed right legs
of the seated, naked from the waist
down, sexless men whose chests
have been wrapped in hair cloth
shirts, tunics, swaddling the afflicted
with no arms, heads bent back to
receive the tainted host, acid rains,
diseased manna, whatever falls from
the scorched wounds of the heavens;
faces, white scars, the same color as
their eyes, once the capacity for sight
has been removed.

Night in the sleepwalker's motel

and the walls are as thin
as rice paper and we

are about to be denied
our dreams by a kind

of music composed for two
sets of dismembered,

weightless hands,
and the ceaseless wheezing

of mating pigeons nesting
in the sagging eaves.

Our room is one of many
identical rooms set inside

this chambered nautilus shell,
walls as hard as the lumps

on the shoulders of a hunch-
backed dwarf, his flaking skin

the snow we cannot see through
when it is time to leave.

Personal Demons: The Artist's Studio

Rendered still life is a Technicolor nightmare:
part feature film, part cartoon with psychic props
made into living images for the artist to play with.
The work place is an interior gymnasium for working
out in artist's smock and track suit, half court games
for one on one confrontations no one not involved
can hope to understand. Real work is an accomplishment
not readily understood. The prime creature we are asked
to imagine sitting with her is dressed in a power suit,
black jacket, red skirt and matching turtle neck.
A weird jackalope welded from something
bipedal making a hoofed thing. Still, somehow,
the creature seems non-threatening, benign, almost serene,
staring straight ahead, though on closer inspection,
the blind left eye suggests something terrible has gone wrong.
A harmless seeming cat climbs on the artist's shoulders,
though one suspects it could turn nasty at the slightest
provocation. Something as nasty as the decapitated
demon head lying on the floor near the stool where
the artist is resting. A stain on the artist's right leg
could be paint or blood, a wound caused by a huge beetle
scuttling across the hardwood floor, or by the demon's sharp fangs,
though only the artist knows for sure what is wounding,
and what is not, what mere frippery, what the vital stuff
no self portrait would be complete without.

The Artist's Reception

This is Frida's Self-Portrait as
a creature in a medieval passion
play rewritten to reflect modern
life. You know the one where she
is naked and strapped onto a flat
board to keep her spine rigid for
easy injections of pain brought
about by needles? Or the one
where she is confined to a leather brace,
a custom-made harness for confinements
in iron maiden devices? Or the one
with removable spikes that can be
used for piercing the immovable body
or can be used to nail her to a tree?
Or the one in this portrait of her
using the last of her life force to
grow a branching object within
and without her, sprouting new leaves,
shaped in the forms of decapitated patrons
of the Arts, government officials, critics,
the same ones who are engaged in
quixotic feats of arms all about
the center piece of her worst,
her most fantastic dreams ever?
You know what kinds of creatures these
are? The ones that Bosch let loose
from a ship of fools to create canvases
so filled with excesses even the creator
must turn away and invent new scenes
of depravity, new layers of hell that exceed

the ones laid out on grids by Dante's brain.
But this painting, this poem, isn't about
Frida, though it was once, when she was
young and alive and could feel the pain
of countless nails being driven deep into
her body, no, now what all this is about
is the sickness, the greed, wars for personal
gain and all the seven deadly sins and a dozen
new ones, all happening around her,
around us, and how we stand and look,
and while we may not agree, we do nothing.

Diego Paints Frida Into Boschland

Frida's portrait is held in place
on the unstable palette by the hands of
cardinals fresh from the celebration
of a Black Mass for uncloseted demons
and demonesses, a gathering aptly served by
unnatural creatures, flying fish whose
predator jaws are held perpetually open
for easy feeding, fast access to Frida's brain.
Her long dangling earring contains
the skeletal remains of disinterred
worshippers, supplicants released
from perpetual días de los muertos,
her other ear a devil's helper newly
released from hell's garden, one
of many pulled from the Calvary
crosses positioned on the black exterior
landscaping Diego uses as a backdrop
cloth, spattered paint, blood of the martyrs
aligned into a Boschian vision of where
worlds collide. As he pauses to consider
this spiritual event horizon, his hands
become unnaturally bent, transformed
into symbolic relics to receive burnt
offerings held just out of reach between
fingers of priests no longer content
with delivering false blessings, absolution,
or indulgences for obscene acts in this life,
despite their being considered normal in the next.
Even frightened into submission the painting
goes on, brush strokes false kisses newly
defining self portraiture, the final tortured frame.

H. Bosch Visits Frida's Wounded Table

She is no longer the woman in white
beset by crows or monkeys.
The jungles of her mind have turned into
a menagerie of fantastic creatures conjured
from a land of the living dead.
A shrunken head on the flat tabletop before
her seems like something kept alive
by electronic impulses, an unseen life force
that determines what is allowed to exist here,
in a world where all the worst imaginings
of horror movies are a matter of fact.
A doll's head, detached from a lifeless torso
brushed clean of any identifying signs, is
caught in a demented voiceless scream so
agonized, all the assembled guests can hear it
although nothing obviously living can.
A stag's misshapen head is perched on
the body of a naked woman whose arms are
the branches fat owls are perched on, wide
eyes observing all the other sinister presences
this gathering has attracted, though the real
danger lies in the slight hands extending
from an unseen place behind the owl bodies,
something that is causing the skeletal shape
to pause in its dance of death to consider
a predatory leap.
Behind this congregation, quite far away,
egg shaped creatures are escaping from this
untended garden of earthly delights to be
swallowed by sentient clouds;

only the artist is unscathed, though it is clear
that she too is no longer human, alive only
in the sense a revenant is, half in this world,
half in another.

Sotheby's Shows Up at Vincent's Death Bed

Which of the figures represents the auction
house? The berobed figure dressed as a cloistered
monk escaped from some horrific imagining
by Breughel the Elder or the master H. Bosch?
Or, might it be the skeletal wraith? Something
clothed in white sheeting suggestive of a nun's habit,
reaching out toward the recumbent artist,
stiff as the flat canvas his life is painted on.
Only Vincent's head is visible on his sick bed.
The lower half of his last self portrait is swathed
in dark painted blankets as he has become
fully possessed by all the inner demons of his
tormented dreams let loose to frolic about
on the larger canvas where he is confronting death.
Could the demon holding bags of gold be the one
he fears most? Or, is it the one holding the damaged
ace of hearts? There is no way of knowing,
though one thing is certain, none of these defilers
of his living legacy care a bit for his suffering or
what it has wrought, beyond mere material objects.
Certainly not the monk with the dangling key
at his waist, rummaging the artist's wood chest
flung open at the foot of the bed, forcibly removing
and examining what was within.
Even as he lies waiting for the end, Vincent knows
all the horrors others felt were delusions of the mind,
were all too real.

Fuck Picasso

Dream creatures from
a cubist's
absinthe nightmare

are the living beasts
that inhabit
the artist's waking

life of death,
body crippled by
palsied limbs,

brittle arthritic bones
bent into useless shapes,

kindling for brain fires,
delirium tremens of
the heart, the scalped head

embodied as these laughing,
once-green
fairies, now demi-gorgons,

parasites that attach
themselves to
the flesh on a fertile

edge of sleep where
nothing is
as real as this

Angels Over a Wheatfield

punk angels in joseph coats
of many colors are levitated
over Vincent's backdrops,
on not exactly a starry night in
progress, but a muddy road
leading nowhere, a confusion of
colors unmistakable as madness,
as a concept rock opera where the dust
of punk angels is joined by hipstreet
junkie priests, wearing cymbals
for halos, and fallen knights of
the templar, their holy robes of
distraction meant to disguise the fact
that they are too stoned for singing,
for effecting a truce, a resurrection
feat; bringing back the artist from
the dead so that he might save himself.

The Locusts, The Plague, The Room

Waiting in
a plagued year
all light is
seen as paint
smears on grimy
panes of glass,
blood blistered skin
unwrapped, each panel
a shaded canvas
of stilled life,
a false dawn
revealed by exposing
bone.

Outside,
on the sloping
ruptured city
streets, locusts
are eating the
buckled pavement,
gas lamps are
being extinguished
by unseen hands;
the sky releasing
a box of heat
containing dreams.

Inside,
even the room
is melting.

The Contours of Fixation

Mute, in the grease
painted night,
a processional is
carrying closed
coffins, raised on
padded shoulders,
back lighted by
hand held torches
casting shadows
like nictitating
membranes, like a
living breathing skin
on unpaved stone,
on blank, unseeing
eyes struck blind
by a mass hysteria
of shared grief.

In a plaza square
before the burial
mound graves
beside the known
contours of fire,
a four piece band
is playing liturgical
jazz, a bald soprano
is singing impossible
half tones and quartered
notes, her face gleaming
in the unnatural
light.

A Distance from the Sea

How the light
breaks stained
glass into tiny
mirrors of the soul

How the rain
filters sound into
sieves straining
notes into particles,
fibers like melodies
that can never be
completely broken
down

How fire
escapes from
the hearth
eating coal from
the mouth of
wooden hoppers,
tasting heat
in the shadowed
corners of
a room

How snow
falls up in
squalls during
certain storms
when prevailing

winds are
right and at
a certain distance
from the sea
all sound is
a kind of song

The Heat in the Room

Heat molds
the unfixed contours
of rooms, bending
shapes into fractured
prisms of unnatural
light creating
the furniture of chaos:
unarmed couches,
backless chairs,
one way doors,
no sash windows,
unframed mirroring glass,
a black hole lit
by lamps exuding
formless shadows,
clouds of dark
that seep through
ceiling cracks
escaping, spreading
as night will

The Trial

The boarding house room is
claustrophobic with so many people,
so close together, asking questions
there are no answers for.
Men in suits represent The Law,
the Men in Robes who preside in
dark places, lit from above by focused
spot lights where interrogations are conducted.
All decision rendered are final,
even before charges are filed, as guilt
is assumed simply by the fact the accused
has been summoned.
All business is conducted at night in
locked rooms where faces of all the bailiffs,
lawyers, inquisitors, and jailors
are hidden by cowls and their voices disguised.
The trial's transcripts are read once,
the judge's gavel signals the proceedings
have begun, thereby simplifying the process
to its basic elements.
Execution seems the logical conclusion
of all that has transpired, but no official
verdict is issued, or recorded, once the rooms
have been emptied of all involved.
There are no gallows, no chambers of horrors
where the final act takes place.
Still the end is a shock, an unexpected deliverance
meted out from behind, by assassins, in black
wielding knives, while others walk before
them speaking of trivial things.

The body of the deceased is left behind for
sky burial outside the castle walls where
other supplicants are making their way to
doors that will not admit them.
The ones who are admitted are guided to
their destination by men in black suits who
speak of trivial matters as they walk not
looking to one side or the other but straight
ahead where a locked room is waiting to be opened.

A Lavender Mist

The man in the studio,
for it must be an artist's workplace,
despite the rude walls,
light filtering through spaces
between misfitted boards,
wall panels, surfaces smeared by a collage
of paints, back splashed from a full-frontal
assault on blank canvas,
brushes hurled in anger, frustration,
spontaneous markings, other images
brushed on, hardened kaleidoscopic pieces,
a true artist's interior

While the man inside scowls,
brushes propped behind his ears,
others resting in old cans from soup, cans,
dog food, baked beans,
vegetables and fruits,
all labels removed
to preserve the integrity
of a (failing) vision;
aided by liquid spirits,
denatured alcohol,
turpentine and linseed oil,
kerosene,
Johnny Walker Red
aged seven years
in a week

The 37 Dreams of Franz Kafka

"Kafka had thirty-seven dreams in his life
and only one concerned sexual activity."
—Anne Carson

are cinematic, as slow motioning,
the lost art of silences filmed,
captioned in white capitals.

Short subjects, he dreams:
a ragtime miming, feels himself
as part of a dissonant farce where
people become animals and animals
become something else.

Escaping from half-lights,
a dream of tigers, of many-faced
beasts woven from the tapestries
of abandoned monastery walls.

On he dreams: the eel dreams,
the arachnid dreams, the one where
scorpions scream, cross-cutting dreams.
unsure of where he is, he proceeds
in the dark, unsure of whether
to read inscriptions on a prison's walls
or to be as blind men are, always
groping for the dark.

2.
Kafka Goes to the Movies

Kafka Goes to the Movies

The Silents
in several cities

at home & abroad

preferring the comedies
to the tragic

No W.B Griffith
Birth of a Nation

No Napoleon
in 100 reels
uncut for Franz

though he does see
a Sentimental Romance
at least seven times

Who knows why?

Always reading
the subtitles

eventually inventing
his own
inner movies

in the darkness
he is loath to share
idle inventions

new works
left incomplete:

Harold Lloyd & His Clock of Doom
Keystone Cops on the Great Wall of China
Buster Keaton's Great Stone Face Undergoes a Metamorphosis
Charlie Chaplin's Starving Artist

The Penal Colony
The Camps

Good Reputation Lies Sleeping 1938
after Alvarez Bravo

All that is needed for a
consecration of a mass is
four tall black candles at each
corner of the not-quite-laid-out
body of the young woman;
a dried skull represents the horned one,
candle lights and sticks of incense further
simulate a rite of passage from the erotic
to the surreal complementing the mostly
naked, trim body swathed in white
bandages, dancer's wraps around the arches
of her feet, upper thighs, and hands, face
set in a euphoric swoon, oblivious to
cactus plants, Aztec idols carved from stone,
dead warrior relics unaware of the black
robed spirits, acolytes of Priapus,
the holiest ghost.

Modern Art

Their heads are disembodied,
Magritte in Baghdad with headscarf
instead of felt hat

Their arms and legs and body
parts are everywhere, stains
on canvas, fields of blue and white
and red.

Their impact is immediate, urgent,
but has no lasting effect unlike
those pieces consigned to museums,
hung on walls, left in dark cellars,
chambers, and forgotten; relics to be
exposed, excavated, placed in context.

Their absence is briefly noted, heard as
a message on airwaves or written of
in newsprint, filmed for international TV;
their names are scrolled in silence at
the end of telecasts; mourned or not,
they have made a mark.

Their cumulative effect is that of a collage,
something by Max Ernst, though not simply
Dada or plainly surreal, but Modern as Art was
before Modern Warfare changed all the Methods,
refined all the Techniques.

Poem Based on a Non-Existent Photograph

Not the dented roofs of the Hudsons,
Packards, Chevrolets parked at city curb,
nor the cracked windshield glass shattered
on impact; not the high over thighs plain
dark skirt, nylon stockings revealed, garter
snaps still intact, nor the face hidden by
hastily applied garment as shield, blonde
permanent wave curls partially visible
where what was meant to cover merely
exposes sudden blemishes, stains; not
the limp white arm dangling beside
the cracked window, fingers spread
as if trying to lift the door lock from outside,
nor the legs, bent at odd angles,
white high heeled shoes still intact amidst
the wreckage, the glass; but the faces
of the pedestrians nearby where she landed:
men, women, children staring, horrified,
a hand to the face, the head, covering
the eyes, suppressing a scream, all of them
more alive than they have ever been before
or will ever be again.

Poem Based on a Non-Existent Photograph

He stands in the yellow painted median,
holding the black lab's metal harness
bar, both man and dog stilled, waiting
as traffic from two facing malls
turns in all directions onto access ramps,
lanes east and west, cross traffic north
and south, into vast parking lots,
blind man and dog part way beyond four
way stop lights, half-way between bus stops,
and seemingly endless stream of cars, buses,
trucks of all sizes, shapes, weights,
hurtling by, heedless of this pair, fixed in
place on diagonal caution lines,
in a breakdown lane for motorists, pedestrians,
and guide dogs, when all systems fail.

Poem Based on Non-Existent Photograph

Votive candles light spaces on the counter
top, the only illumination inside blackout
darkened saloon. The drinkers hunched,
leaning against the bar, barely more than shadows,
shapes, etched into a plate glass window,
clouded backbar mirrors, behind a skyline
of molded plastic bottle-stoppers,
just short of an event horizon, rooted behind
beer tap markers, wooden stick handles,
these grave markers for the regulars;
their black shadowed eyes, their pale as death faces
rimmed in fading corollas of insufficient light.

Poem Based on Non-Existent Photograph

Black magic marker stains on white
tiled subway walls deliver the message:
SATAN RULES HERE-
DIAL 666 FOR A GOOD TIME--
words of wisdom largely ignored by
the subterranean creatures of night,
passing through here on the way to
somewhere else, unheeded by the indigent one
reclining here, head slumped onto his chest,
worn and pilled polyester pants and ragged suit
jackets sizes too small, fitted over bulging layers
of stained shirts, rumpled brown paper bag
close at hand, torn at the bottle neck revealing label:
CRAZY HORSE MALT--
40 ounces to going nowhere man, waiting
for the big sleep amid the dust and debris
of this disused and mostly deserted place,
one stop away from Hell's Kitchen.

Poem Based on a Non-Existent Photograph

Seated in the overhanging awning shadow
on cracked concrete sidewalk, legs stretched
out before him, disruptive to people passing by,
his detaching rubber soled sneakers lacking
laces, loose tongues flapping; rolled at the bottom
khaki colored Dickies, soiled by motor oil,
food stuffs and filth; frayed woolen jacket over
a t-shirt: New York Yankees World Champions 1999,
a hole revealing gray chest hair.
His unwashed, spastic hands gesticulate,
conducting an unseen chorus of accusing voices,
whispering "My son, make thyself merry
and laugh, laugh, laugh-----"

Poem Based on a Non-Existent Photograph

The race track crowd remains hushed
at the railing, some leaning over near
the finish line to see what happens next,
others turning away knowing the inevitable
result, not caring to see as the surface is re-graded,
horse hoof divots smoothed away, raked-
over except for the largest ones near where
the carrier van is backing up, where a
temporary white screen is being unfolded,
while the odds on the electric tote board
remain fixed, win, place and show spaces
blank, no dollar value affixed, all in
suspension, all awaiting the single pistol shot
that will not signify the start of another
high stakes race.

Poem Based on a Non-Existent Photograph

The older woman passing by, clutching her handbag
to her chest with both gloved hands, seems more
horrified than amazed at the sight of the gaunt
woman who has just gone by, hopping on her left
leg, worn polyester pants stained about the cuff
of the ambulatory leg, the other held straight behind,
foot encased in a tattered moccasin, unmatched to
the other, encased as it is in a shoe more sensible for hopping;
fake fur winter jacket to just below the waist,
its white neck now gray, her hair streaked gray,
white, and nicotine yellow, all her vital
personal possessions contained in three
over-the-shoulder denim bags in lieu of a purse,
oblivious to the onlookers dressed for church or shopping,
as the one nearby her is, staring in the wake of mad woman
hopping, unsure whether to speak, cry out, or to run.

Non-Existent Photograph in the Manner of Diane Arbus

features three lunatics in white camisoles,
strapped to the backs of metal chairs,
heads twisted as far as they can be,
neck muscles tensed, animal eyes wild,
rolled most of the way inside swollen
hooded lids, black from lack of sleep,
cheeks puffed in places, raw where they
have scratched, bruised following a primal
struggle against restraint, foam leaking
from the edges of their cracked lips,
thin lines of blood mixing in; if they scream
their mouths will be taped shut, after leather grips
are affixed, something to bite instead of a tongue,
sometimes even these do not prevent the damage
that can be done; one photo is only a small part
of the story.

Non-Existent Photograph in the Manner of Brassaï

In the gas-lit village, all the faces
are painted white, smeared greasepaint
for unspeakable people, unnatural acts.
The half-dead and the naked, along with
the might-as-well-be dead, are stumbling
down slick wet cobblestones, arm in arm,
impelled by an inner music provided by
a hopped-up jazz band improvising
notes never heard before. They are
sight reading sheet music for the deaf
and the blind, whom they lead into dead-
ending alleyways, storm sewers, all the night
shelters/haunts of the improvident.
All these rented-by-the-hour bodies
lying in wait, above ground and below,
are the poster people for a village of the damned,
their unnaturally wide eyes affecting
a sinister glow. They live where the candles
burn down from both ends. Meeting in
the middle, these night people rising,
their lips still on fire.

A Non-Existent Photograph in the Manner of Lisette Model

Inside the fortune telling booth,
an opalescent ball balanced on
a wooden stand, a well-worn
deck of playing cards stacked
nearby on a threadbare Oriental
throw. An enormous woman
of indeterminate old age, fingers
fat as small sausages, wears
gold plated rings, imitation pearls,
polished semi-precious stone bracelets,
her right hand absently caressing
the ball she claims to divine
the future in. The folds of her bulk are
enhanced by musty scents and sweat
stained garments, her gray-at- the-roots
hair contained by a bulky swath
of colored scarves.
Her hooded eyes are sunk deeply into
her skull, her swollen lips pursed,
shaded by a semi-gloss of dark red lipstick.
When she speaks a multiplicity of chins
move, suggesting decades of smoking
and drinking hard liquors. She says,
"How would you like your future told?
Through the cards or as seen in
the magic crystal ball?"

Non-Existent Photograph in the Manner of Louis Hine

The man of indeterminate age is
dressed in Goodwill castoffs,
his lazy right eye rolling about
in the damaged-by-fire socket.
The left eye is fused in place,
focused on something always just above
or just beyond, where you are now.
He is leaning on a rude crutch made
from tree limbs and padded
with soiled and tattered rags.
One pant leg is rolled up, knotted,
tied off as a tourniquet would be,
as if there were a limb there that needed
tending. His right arm missing as well,
shirt similarly adjusted to accommodate
what remains. On the ground near
where he stands, a hand painted sign says:
WOUNDED. On the ground by the sign,
a bent and dented metal cup soliciting
pity tips he needs to live on.

Non-Existent Photograph in the Manner of Weegee

The afterhours bar is home
for many circus workers, freaks,
off hours away from work,
dressed for being out in public.
The Incredible Thin Man wears
a shabby suit sans tie, felt hat
creased in places hats are not
meant to be creased, is leaning over
the bar, cradling draft beer the way
a tree limb leans against storm winds.
The Strong Man wears a tight black shirt,
split at the side where muscles bulge,
sleeves cut off revealing tattoos, slogans,
ports of origin and escape, his bald head
covered by a Watchman cap, shot glasses
for boilermakers waiting on the bar for
the beers. The Fat Lady in a muumuu
dress, a flowered tent, with cut outs in all
the appropriate places, a secret pocket inside
where she stores cash, snacks, and sipper bottles
concealed from all but the dwarf. He stands
on the bar stool nearby, exercising his god given right
to be the loudest, brashest, most obnoxious
member of the troupe, awash, as he normally is,
in a small sea of alcohol, always demanding more,
and would always be easily ignored,
were it not for the Strongman.

A Non-Existent Photograph in the Manner of Mary Ellen Mark

These freaks of nature are not
something salvaged for display
as just another roadside distraction.
Instead, they are real life tragedies
of inbreeding, hard drug use,
and alcohol abuse, born into some kind
of polluted gene pool. Their withdrawal
from the womb is from their direct
connection with all the drugs
and alcohol they will need to avoid
hideous convulsions, nightmares,
tremors, all part of an ordeal of
endurance they will face from first
days of life. Years later, weaned
from others' habits, the luckier ones
will have attention deficit disorders,
autistic lives, that will make them
incapable of learning.
Others will be afflicted with maladies
bearing names such as: Gigantism,
Micro and Macrocephalism,
Hydrocephalism and crudely called:
water-heads, pinheads, fatheads.
They will always be larger or smaller than life,
doomed to watch an endless loop of
meaningless cartoons on television,
the only images that hold their attention.

A Non-Existent Photograph in the Manner of Man Ray

Superimposition is the technique
twinning a naked woman with
the image of a freestanding grand-
father clock, faces overlapping,
marking the hour on her cheek,
minutes on the bridge of her nose,
the long swaying of the clock wand,
a blur spanning her legs, time-lapsed,
to preserve her in-question modesty.

Smiling, her face is ringed by Roman
numerals. She holds a piper's flute,
is seen as poised to play an air,
a suitable preamble for a romp in
the fields, or is the image an odd,
Dadaist, visual pun? A suggestive
joke later known as Naked Woman
Dancing to the Music Of Time?

Non-Existent Photograph in the Manner of Lupow

Near dark, they are the scavengers with
metal detectors working the shoreline,
waving their instruments over the smooth
sea swept sand, the moss tangles, beach junk...
They are almost identical twins: The Tweedledee
& Tweedledum of Brooklyn, sporting
faded, once midnight-blue baseball caps,
they have pulled down low over their foreheads
to just over their eyes. The scrolled letter B,
on the crown, is no longer white but a kind of
grit gray like their shrunken t-shirts,
stretched to the limit over beer keg bellies.
Their cut-off black denim shorts
are sliding down toward their groins beneath
so much unsupportable girth. Their rubber flip flops,
are minimal protection from disgusting beach refuse:
used condoms, beached jelly fish, medical
waste: syringes, bandaging, plasma sacks.
Their unlit fat cigars, clenched tight in the corners
of their mouths, are more chewed than smoked.
In the last phantom light, before the after-work
influx to the bars for the game of the week,
where major deals are discussed and cut, they are
hard at their work, on the beach, where all
the unexcavated treasure waits.

This Is Not Art
: an assemblage

"The Americans call photography an art. They have galleries, institutions, exhibitions. But what I'm doing is not art." Don McCullin

Cholera victim. Eyes rolled back into her head. Cradled in arms of her husband as an offering to Death.

Shabby woman of no particular age. Standing in her, three-rungs-below-hell, dwelling. "Rats the size of cats," her son says. Whoring is a way of life here. You have to eat. So does the boy with no-future eyes.

An American soldier in Hue city. During the offensive. Throwing a grenade amid the ruins toward an unseen enemy. Seconds before his arm is blown off by a sniper's bullet. Before another soldier takes his place. Throws a grenade. Is shot. Before another man is ordered forward.

Three heavily armed, cocky young American soldiers in South East Asia. Their captive forced to his knees, arms trussed behind his back, rope around his neck like a leash. Eyes blindfolded with a dirty white rag. The village behind them about to burn.

Three blind black women fast walking in bare feet past heavily armed guerrilla force on the last days of the Smith regime in Rhodesia.

American army chaplain lifting an confused, dazed old woman from bombing raid rubble.

A face-only portrait of a starving boy in Biafra.

The ordered and the disordered.

Oh, the Humanity.

For Francesca Woodman Whenever I Find Her

Your spirit body knows no boundaries,
not walls nor ceilings, not window glass
nor hard wood doors, though even you
can't defy gravity.

Even your most intimate seeming portraits
have no real people in them, blurs, yes, smears,
maybe, of course, where something solid should be.

The lumps in the torn wallpaper contain
a body inflated with decay. The kind of
ruin only forgotten objects can display.
Even the Exit signs in the background
have no internal light to guide you from
one unsafe place to another.

Fear of falling is a subject you can only
explore once. It's not the falling that
gets you, it's the impact.

3

How We Live Now

Remains Unsuitable for Viewing
after Charles Simic

The paperwork said.

The coffin duly marked as such, as well.
We wonder who made the decision for us
And why.

It wasn't as if he'd been struck blind
and sent to clear a minefield.

If we could see what was left inside
we might conclude otherwise.

Clearing the minefields.
One man is never enough.

Self-Portrait of the Disease That Is Killing Me

The canvas of the self shows:
skin peeled away, revealing
an anatomy lesson in progress,
rib cage broken, all the organs
exposed, Vesalius's open wound.

This is not an autopsy, per se,
but a prelude of things to come,
variations on an ode, imitations
of mortality on a timed scale.

An appendage is not welcome
here, may be as malignant as
thwarted desire, a knot of
wounds bound to a broken frame.

The health of the sick is
measured inside with daubs
of flustered color, free floating
pain that resists the painterly eye.

Self-Portrait with Forensic Evidence

The design is something
from another age: alternating
stripes once wallpapers, several
different shades of old, fading,
age spotted, yellowing, veined and
cracked as the house settled, water leaked
or paste dried out; pieces peeling,
curling as they unfurled, whole panels
at a time, neglected, webbed with dust,
spiders nesting, an encroachment
of decay unchallenged. This place,
once a home, now derelict, almost
totally forgotten, but for the defining
incident. These new scattershot
patterns applied to wall and allowed
to dry as stains, no one would confuse
as a new, experimental, ornamental
work in progress, not even the master
surrealists, post-modernists, futurists,
scientists who come here to analyze;
to determine methodologies, motives,
secrets of the form.

How We Live Now

after Georgia O'Keeffe

A gas mask super-
imposed on
a desert landscape

a flat yellow-brown
mustard cloud
fetid as an olive-green
boil rising

bleached by the sun
deadwood branches
stark white fingers
pointing to the sky

Reno 1949
after Lisette Model

Dark sunglasses do not betray what she
might be feeling, the way an application
of too much lipstick does.
She is not in town for the races or the tables,
though she bets on horses, plays the slots,
rolls the dice, but whether she wins or loses
makes no difference, it is the playing,
the killing of time, that matters.
Smoking cigarettes at the edge of an in-
ground pool, she turns the pages of High
Society magazines, but retains nothing of
what she reads, fills ashtrays with half-
smoked cigarettes, the imprint of her lipstick
a blood red smear, a memorial to all the time
spent establishing her residency requirement here.
Night times are no different, only the places
where she maintains her home base of inactivity
are changed; the strength of her libations increased
so that by full moonrise, as the new light astonishes,
she is a wild woman of the dunes in flimsy silk
nightwear, the sand filtering down all about her.

Donnie with Baby and Cows
after photo by Shelby Lee Adams

The cows look superimposed
beneath this makeshift shelter:
part flying saucer, part mold
and moss covered inverted metal
dish, receiving transmissions
from above and funneling them
directly into the ground through
metal support poles. Maybe the poles
siphon these random signals into
the irregular barriers of an electrified
fencing, or the cored hot water heater,
or even the large stump roots decorated
with cast-aside exhaust system pipes,
junked car parts and farm effluvia.
If they are, Donnie isn't telling.
He is too busy jury rigging stuff,
making sure nothing, even vaguely
reusable, will ever go to waste.
What do the cows care? They are
among the dumbest creatures on God's
good earth, a sentiment shared,
no doubt, by farmer Donnie, cradling
a babe in arms, both smiling for
the camera; a family album keepsake
or is the picture to be digitally
re-mastered and broadcast to warn off
all the others still in outer space?

The Cockfighter
after Shelby Lee Adams

His face is so bloated
it is difficult to decide
whether he is pre-
pubescent or sexually
mature, if his grotesque gut
is the result of a genetic
trait, or a life of indolence,
gluttony, & Pabst Blue
Ribbon Beer consumption.
Nearby are super-sized televisions
for monitoring football,
NASCAR and ESPN's
National High School
Cheerleading competition,
while he is waited on by
a woman of similar size and
tastes: a plus size giantess
wearing a Carolina Panthers
football jersey number 69
and little else. Everything he
needs in life is at his fingertips:
a remote control, an iced
cold brew, and a cell phone
for calling in last minute action
before kick, tip off, first pitch...
He never leaves the house
except to enter the prize cock
in high stakes blood sport.
Then he is chauffeured in

the family heirloom: a near mint
two-tone DeSoto car,
which he stands beside in his
traveling duds: cutoff shorts,
feed & seed cap, and filthy
bloodstained t-shirt, none
of which remotely fit, in
polar opposition to the proud
cock he holds: sleek, well groomed,
and dignified, a true warrior.

Peggy and Albert
after Shelby Lee Adams

They look like a new
age American Gothic,
posed before their life
transforming modern
appliance for farm and
home; the family satellite
dish. She is scowling,
dressed in her going-to-town,
pressed black and white,
polka dot dress. Her scrawny
arms are liver spotted and
whittled down to sinew,
nothing but bone and flesh,
after years of hard working
the fields, house, gardens,
child rearing…
He holds the empty nest
replacement: a miniature
collie. His lined, pinched,
perpetually sour face
is shaded by Agway store
cap and dark glasses. His new
dungarees are rolled into huge
cuffs for trapping dust, lint,
and the odd dropped nickel.
His never-stepped-in-shit shoes
are polished for the special
occasion of a snap shot,
his fresh from-a- package,

Fruit of the Loom t-shirt is
still creased on this late Fall
afternoon. You can almost feel
the transmissions, that multiplicity
of channels in the dish, cycling
through the early morning
hours, programming pulled in
from faraway images and sounds,
all those emanations silently
being absorbed.

Jane, sitting for a portrait
after Shelby Lee Adams

in her wedding dress, is so
old and close to crossing over
to the other side, her picture
will be called "Terminal Woman
with Mourning Dove." Wasted
flesh, pale, yellowing, paper thin
skin over bones that have no marrow,
blue veins carrying liquid chemicals,
desiccants, through a body all feeling
has been leached from.
This white wedding is with
old Mr. Bones, who does not care
if there is actual consummation,
a sexual union, to bind them as man
and wife, knowing their marriage
transcends the body, and is for all
time. This second wedding is so
completely unlike her first one.
Then, what the flesh offered
was all they could afford and they spent
it often, and unwisely, bearing children
they could not care for or keep track of.
The artist asks Jane if she has any
final wishes to impart before he
completes the portrait but she relays
none, having been struck dumb by disease.
If she could have spoken, "No",
that would have been the last word
to escape her lips.

Ray with Sister and New Bride 1980
after Shelby Lee Adams

"Marry them young, before they
get all wore out." Must be the backwoods
philosophy that Ray subscribed to.
His blonde child wife is almost skeletal,
barely post-pubescent, has a protruding
forehead and prominent facial bones,
containing eyes already dull and losing
their vitality. Ray's sister is the hefty one,
the one he really wants, crouching near
the love-birds, displaying a wicked overbite
instead of a smile for the camera.
Ray is scowling for this family portrait,
wearing his finest soiled clothes,
the ones without tatters or tears, clearly
the least mentally deficient of the group,
the one destined to be the lead idiot
in a land of the mentally challenged.
His shy familiar, a former bloody
fraternal twin, is skulking about in
the background, lurking, almost unnoticed,
until he emits a lunatic laugh,
one used for all occasions; for weddings or
for celebrating the changing phases of the moon.

Annie's Kitchen 1992
after Shelby Lee Adams

reveals the toiling of a lifetime,
pots scrubbed free of leftovers/
spillage; all the outside surfaces,
veneers, completely removed,
dented, pitted, warped totally out
of shape, molded into something
original, something unique, but by
no means new. This is Annie's
work space and she is not chained
to her gas stove but doesn't seem
able, or inclined, to move far from
this space. Her body is bent by work
and deficiency diseases, her arms
clutching her stomach, not for warmth
or comfort, but to cradle the pain
that is reflected in her hard eyes,
along with the fatigue. All her
misshapen features seem carved from
stone: oft broken nose, deep sunken eyes
burrowed within fat bulges of skin,
irregular cheek bones, chin slanted
to one side, lips cut into that expressive
face, barely concealing last remains
stumps of teeth; her once floral patterned
house dress buttoned in the wrong order,
lopsided, more sad than comic,
because, who cares? Not the man
with his huge hands resting on his hips?
And certainly not Annie.

Nora's Bedroom
after Shelby Lee Adams

is a forgotten childhood storage
room, abandoned in mid-collection,
all the indiscriminate oddments assembled
and left behind: Ceramic Elvis likenesses,
wall hangings, stuffed for cuddling
dolls, Howdy Doody rubber puppet
heads, marionettes without strings, Barbies
and Shirleys, all arrayed in rows, amid
family outing pictures from between wars,
vases with dried flowers, shelves of knick-
knacks. Here too the perfume bottles, cameos,
paperweights so covered with grime and dust,
turning them over unleashes a storm of snow
and gunk, in this place where childhood's end
was preserved, and sealed as a time capsule
of disconnected junk and disorder,
where Nora's face is the last object noticed,
staring out from the tarnished mirror, her eyes
stealing pieces of your mind, one useless object
at a time.

The Flyswat: The Napier Family at Home
after Shelby Lee Adams

The hole in the wall, edged by
cardboard is not a window,
but a mirror. The son with dark
tarnished eyes, is staring into,
sees the flyswat hanging dead center
on the wall opposite wall, sees
the glass divided into unequal pieces,
used for looking at lost worlds and
fading pictures from old circulars
that serve as wall coverings
where wall boards gap and make-do
newspaper fillers fail as barriers
to inclement weather and winter winds.
The toothless old man on the porch
outside wears worn-for-generations
overalls. Will not tolerate insect life,
always keeping the family weapons
handy for emergency use, along
with the more substantial ones, those
double barreled shotguns he does not
hesitate to use when the spirit moves,
even if it his own kind he is shooting at.

Tammy
after Shelby Lee Adams

Even at seven, standing in her
backyard, blonde hair uncombed,
her eyes are hard and already
focusing on a place well beyond
where she is at. Her hand-me-down dress
is filthy, dark in places as the permanent
bruises forming under her eyes
that no makeup will cover in her twenties.
She will already be more dead than alive,
jailhouse tattoos on both arms,
still dressed in filthy clothes;
though her eyes will be less intense,
harder to focus on the place way beyond
where she has been looking, at nowhere,
that place, more real than any place she
has ever been.

The Napier Family 1989
after Shelby Lee Adams

Their family portrait shows only
three of sixteen offspring. Shows
the boys who survived into their twenties
for a family shoot, not bothering
with formalities like shirts, all the better
to show off their grotesque scars:
a belly so disfigured, it is difficult
to imagine how it got that way—
a growth removed by home surgery,
anesthetized with alcohol;
or maybe through acts of violence,
like the ones that removed so many of
their kin from the picture: the son shot
by the father, a daughter poisoned by
relatives, another son shot by a brother,
others killed by strangers, law enforcement
agents. All these local legends story-
tellers dwell on, concentrating on
the more amusing aspects of their drunken
stunts: the son who has his address
tattooed on his knuckles and hand so
the sheriffs will know whose people
he belongs to, where to drop him off
when the sentence is done, or sooner,
if the verdict was death and the alcohol
black out permanent. It is the son with a
home-styled haircut who thrusts his head
into the shot at the last moment that attracts
the most attention, a wicked smile on his

profiled face, a knife scar prominent
stretching all the way from his lip the length
of his jaw, telling all that you will ever need
to know about the family lineage; the ones
gone and the few who remain.

Rose Lee and Junior's Wedding
after Shelby Lee Adams

Theirs is a marriage made in some
Kentucky backwoods, consecrated by
the general store owner/local preacher/
justice of whatever,
pronouncing them man and wife,
then selling them pints of liquor for their
after-the-marriage ceremony celebration
though neither of them is anywhere near
the legal drinking age. And off they
would go, swilling booze in the front
seat of Junior's hotrod top down convertible,
its back seat the site of many a consummation,
now a repository for empty container
violations as they speed down one lane
unpaved roads, drinking up the miles
until it's time to refuel, returning to the one
pump station where the day began, new
supplies of liquid refreshments acquired
to continue the stated mission of getting
drunk on the first night of wedded bliss life.
Junior ordering up a fifth of Black Jack Daniels
and a fifth of *agua caliente*, rotgut Tequila,
or at least that was the plan before the
accelerator got stuck, wheeling them out
of control at something like 105 mph on
bald front tires, spraying smoke and gravel,
once the brakes were finally applied, and
the gas pedal unstuck, literally ditching them

on the side of what passed for a road,
in this one-horse, one-store, no-account
poor excuse for a town, in nowhere Kentucky;
bride and groom unharmed-- though, as Junior
later said, "It might be a spell before Rose Lee's
hair lies down flat and straight where it belongs."
and his too, though he'd never admit it.

The Crouched Ones, 1934

after Alvarez Bravo

'the eye thinks,
the throat sees,
the sight touches,
the words burn'
     Octavio Paz

Pure fire is transparent, liquid
combusts at the lips, the drinkers'
heads hidden in semi-darkness,
almost invisible, bend to receive
clear offerings bartered for with
centavos, pesos, meal money
for los niños, their hardscrabble
infants left with rags for clothing,
and dried maize for food, as their
elders, these men, consider los
gusanos, the worms floating in
a suspension of mescal, mescalito,
to be eaten at the end, fought over,
killed for, an elusive prize for these
haphazard dreamers, dreaming the
waking dream of sleep, sueños de
los muertos; in the dark behind
the bar anything is possible.

Firefighters 1935
after Alvarez Bravo

They are dressed in outrageous uniforms:
jackets in a fabric like burlap,
cut several sizes too big,
pants they must walk on to move,
hands covered by oven mitts,
heads covered by potato sacks
with small eye holes well above
their foreheads, an outfit that might
be useful for warding off heat
or blending in with adobe walls,
in case their transformation has
been completed, so that they
may be sacrificed to alien invaders
in a Grade B movie.
Which movie would they fit in?
The atomic ray- exposed,
mutant creatures, one with ants
now the size of school buses,
the one with outsized tarantulas,
iguanas, prehistoric toads, invading
border towns just this side of the desert.
Or the movie with the guys in red uniform
tops, clothes of doom that marked
the wearers as walking dead men
by the next reel.
But this photo is taken in 1935,
years before the first atomic tests,
red menace scares, TV melodramas,

huge spikes in cancer tumor deaths,
and these men have a real job to perform,
crippled by their clothes, as they approach
the scene, the fires that await them.

Threshold 1947

after Alvarez Bravo

"The river like a stone
to drown in."
Eric Basso

Tentative, her curled toes
refuse to touch what is spilled

by the threshold, a riffling
puddle where she sees something

unknowable, a mirroring,
perhaps a reflective light,

an interior landscape of nether
worlds, recent arrivals from a city

of dreams; the spill appears to be water
to the eye, but the mind sees something

forbidden, an essence of the un-
redeemable, blood of the future past.

Day of the Dead 1932
after Alvarez Bravo

The object she is holding cradled
in her lap is a formed from sugar
skull. the word AMOR, is carved
into the cavity above where the smiling,
toothless mouth has been rendered
in death's favorite color, white.
The skull's smile mirrors her own,
suggesting this memento mori is
from her beloved, is an auspicious
gift on a day of the dead, when the unseen
spirits are roaming the earth, released on
for one day in order to bestow blessings
on the living by saying, "After your time
among the living, now, you will join us,
walking the earth. Your cries of recognition,
recall our last breaths, the fearsome
agony of leaving the known, for another
place, far beyond feelings of pleasure
and of pain. Your time will be filled
with many blessings and when you must
depart, there will be no need to feel regret
or sorrow." Her face is beatific,
filled with radiance and love,
a joy beyond words. That night,
as she lies in the arms of her lover,
the skull will be the last object she sees
before her eyes are closed.

1924

after Alvarez Bravo

"The bush with holes was burning
cannibals remember to eat,
all thoughts are made up."
                Norma Cole

"Does the barber shave himself."
                N. Cole

The man seated on a low stool,
leaning forward, head bent, limp
shouldered, pale clothes blending
with high adobe wall, pocked with bullet
holes. Maybe he is listening to songs
from firing squad days, pop tunes,
symphonies of mass execution, that
outlast death, tone poems of trans-
migrating souls, long after the rainbows
of death are white washed away.
What is most real is the fact of
another figure, a larger man in black,
not of the assassination trade, no pistol
aimed at the base of the sitting one's brain,
but a worker scissoring hair from the seated
one, maintaining a posture of dominance
and control, a standard issue black blind-
fold dangling from his pants pocket kept
handy for binding about the head of
the accused or the neck to be shaved,
as the time and the place demands.

The Eclipse
after Alvarez Bravo

"The sun does not
love although
It's sympathy is blinding."
                Norma Cole

She is holding the black
cloth draped across her eyes
behind the white laundry hung
out to dry. The cloth is for
protecting her eyes from intense,
direct sunlight. What she
fears is what will never be
seen, the sensitive insides of
eyes struck blind, live parasites
crawling within, eating their way out.
The pain is intolerable.
When she turns away, from the light,
she no longer able to see, and tiny
scars are burning into her head
where her eyes once were.
The black cloth she was holding,
is like the crepe that is used for covering
mirrors on a day of death.

S. Plachy's Dachau-Germany 1985

Striped prison suits
hung from ceiling on
black wire hangers,
an unexpected super-
imposition of curtained
windows as luminous
as backward reflections
on threadbare cloth;
such strange twinning,
these factory made
familiars, united
by their emptiness.

Wladyslaw Szpilman, "The Pianist", with his siblings 1914

This is the Real Lost Generation:
Warsaw Jews in their youth,
posed for a studio portrait,
when anything was possible but
nothing was.

The Vertical Journey: Six Movements Within the Heart of the City

"me and that old woman sorrow...."

In bumfucked night, down Bowery
bottlenecks, under Coney Island
boardwalks, nighttown rings, lower
than hell, sideshows and freakouts,
money lenders extending the temples
of greed, group groping the far edges
of sex, everything saleable has a price,
even the freaks: Tattoo Jack, the masked
man, outstaring everyone, even Death;
Uncle Sam of the deadbeat alleyways,
flag suits and top hats he hides his product in,
no one too young or too innocent to be recruited,
dope is dope and money is money, one comes
with the other, who cares who buys as long
as the cash is green; Willie Mack, sage of
the wilderness, house of the risen sun pad
under an EL, all the way downtown,
rathole cellar dump filled floor to ceiling with
two dollar ninety eight cent jugs, labels that
read PARADISE, something offered, never received,
nearby baby carriages for the dead soldiers,
the headless dolls, all the junk that fits,
coffee cans filled with butts, lost keys,
dead insects, roaches, "anything once living
can be food", so sayeth Madam Sandra,
the ancient housefrau, everyone's suburban
grandmother with her all-seeing black ball,

three dollar sessions revealing all but what people
most want to know: how and when; white cellar
rooms in Bellevue, clean sheets for the deceased,
toe tags for an unknown man, hanging loose for all to see.

Street Theater NYC

after Amy Arbus

Their outfits suggests
dressing up for street
theater/festivities such
as the mermaids of Coney
Island, though what their
theme might be is open
to serious questioning.
One is a sheer dress
made from locks and keys
held in place by decorative
bicycle chains. Another a mandarin
length, press-on nails ensemble,
a kind of Boy George clone
out of place and time.
Nearby, the key lady, a turn of
the last century love child,
spawn of 60's hippie-diva
Melanie, in search of the mythical
repository of lost bike locks
and all-weather wicks for holding
candles in the rain at the next
bogus Woodstock revival,
a festivity Boy/Girl George &
his/her culture club/crew would
arrive at too stoned to notice
much of anything not part of
this all too soft parade.

Subnormals Dressed for the Halloween Masquerade

after Diane Arbus

"The photographs appear to be documents of a world we've never seen or imagined before-one with its own ritual and icons, its own games and fashions and codes of conduct-which, for all its strangeness, is at the same time hauntingly familiar and, in the end, no more or less unfathomable than our own."
Doon Arbus

They are the children of God, not quite
forgotten in their late adult confinement,
all old and young forever, before their un-
natural time, dressed for the Untitled Halloween
Dance, the Fall Ball 196- whatever. These
princesses and ballerinas, cowboys and athletes,
women decked out in taffeta gowns, and dime store
lace, those confined to wheelchairs clutching
their evening bag in one hand, and
the masquerade mask in the other, only their
smiles fully revealed. The ambulatory holding
strap handles of paper bags, against
their waists, full face masks adjusted slightly
askew, as they stand or sit for group portraits
on dull gray afternoons in the institutional
courtyards. The males fully uniformed as well,
no weapons or implements of play war or games
nearby to interfere with the primary function
of all this dressing up: Trick or treating door to door,
in the community, or on the open ward-- it makes
no difference.

Blow Up
after photos by Don McCullin

This is the city after
the riots, at any time,
any place where red
brick row houses are
still standing, in working
class slum, walkup front
doors and windows boarded
closed: KEEP OUT
KEEP AWAY BY POLICE
ORDER, written in white
paint, long streaks trailing
down from rude letters,
overprinted in red:
FUCK OFF. No longer
children, preteen boys
sharing a smoke, sitting on
upper tenement steps, angry,
defiant, sullen, looking toward
where latest action is, car bombs
and Molotov Cocktails in
the mornings instead of
breakfast. Looking away,
they are already bored, now
that London burning.
This is how they live now.

The Future

> "So our hope lies in a world without hope, governed by Satan."
>
>   Ake Edwardson, Sun and Shadow

"Neighborhood girl, 8, killed
by stray bullet while riding
her new bicycle."
The news article said.

Police canvassed the neighborhood
looking for leads but no one saw
anything, though everyone seemed
to have heard the shots. Were on
the street seconds later, and were glad
to appear on local TV offering
opinions about all the things they
didn't see.

Weeks later a thirteen year old
boy was arrested for the crime.
Said he felt bad about the little
girl. "I wasn't trying to shoot
no little girl. I was trying to off
someone else. She just be in the way."

Asked where he got the gun,
he confessed it wasn't his, was,
in fact, a community gun, that anyone
could use, if they had to, as long as
they put it back where it was to be
hid when they were done.

Said, he had to wait until he was 16
to get his own gun but guessed, now,
he'd never get one.

The Year in Review in Pictures:
an abridged selection from the New York Times

"Every war is ironic because every war is worse than expected."
Paul Fussell 1924-2012

American sailors with captured Somali pirates
Thousands of people return home after ten years of war, Darfur
Frozen child, refugee camp, Afghanistan
Man on fire running, New Delhi
Nik Wallenda highwire walking over Niagara Falls Gorge
Kim Jong-Un reviewing the troops, May Day, North Korea
Human skull and bones mass grave, Mazar I Sharif, Afghanistan
Pussy Riot in Moscow Courtroom cage
Wendy Maritza Rodriguez after seeing the corpse of a relative
Forty-six new graves cut in a field, Krymsk, Russia
Statue of Blessed Virgin Mary after the fire, Breezy Point, Queens
Aerial View of Manhattan showing blackout of the city after Sandy
Israeli family braced for incoming rockets near Ashdod
Palestine residents clearing debris, Gaza City, the next day
Night in Syria after airstrike in Aleppo
26 killed, 20 children, 6 adults, Newton, Connecticut elementary school massacre (not shown)

About the Author

ALAN CATLIN is retired from his unchosen career in the "Hospitality Industry". During that time he worked as a proof checker, crowd control expert, clean up man, the grim sweeper, bartender, college tavern manager, management trainee for a national restaurant, night manager of a chain hotel, banquet bartender and coordinator, night club head bartender, nightclub beverage manager, responsible for ordering, stocking and selling over a million dollars, in 70's dollars, and finally, both part time night guy, then, full time day guy in an Irish tavern. During his six decade publishing career, he has released countless chapbooks and full length books of prose and poetry. Among those are *Effects of Sunlight on Fog* (Bright Hill), *Self-Portrait of the Artist Afraid of His Self-Portrait* (March Street) *American Odyssey and Wild Beauty* (Future Cycle Press), *Blue Velvet* (winner of 2017 Slipstream Chapbook Contest), *Hollyweird* (Nightballet Press), *Walking Among Tombstones in the Fog* (Presa Press) and *Last Man Standing* (Lummox Press).

For the full Dos Madres Press catalog:
www.dosmadres.com